DON'T GO BROKE!

The Truth Behind NC Long Term Care Planning

Jeffrey G. Marsocci, Esq.

Domestic Partner Publishing, LLC

Note Regarding Information

As with any product, it is important to be clear about its intended purpose and use to avoid any misunderstandings. Specifically with writings about legal issues, it is noted that these materials are not a substitute for competent legal counsel. The contents of this book are instead written to provide information about Care Assistance and Long Term Care problems and opportunities, and it is designed for general educational purposes only. The contents of this book are not to be construed as legal advice, and no attorney-client privilege exists between the reader and the author and/or publisher. In addition, laws change frequently, and therefore you also are urged to speak with an attorney about changes in the law that may affect you. *In order to implement the strategies outlined in this book, speak to an attorney.*

Circular 230 Disclosure: To ensure compliance with requirements imposed by the Internal Revenue Service, unless specifically indicated otherwise, any tax advice contained in this communication (including any accompanying literature) was not intended or written to be used, and cannot be used, for the purpose of avoiding tax-related penalties or promoting, marketing, or recommending to another party any tax-related matter addressed herein. For specific legal advice, you are urged to contact an attorney in your state or jurisdiction.

The stories contained herein have been fictionalized in whole or in part to convey some of the benefits of good Care Assistance Planning, show the detriments of poor planning or no planning at all, and/or to protect the identities of the innocent and not so innocent.

About the Author

Jeffrey G. Marsocci was born in Fort Worth, Texas, and raised in Lincoln, Rhode Island, where he graduated from Mount Saint Charles Academy High School. He received his Bachelor's degree in Business from Hofstra University, and two years later earned his law degree from the same university.

In 2004, he received a Certificate Degree in Non-Profit Management from Duke University, and has earned his Legal Master of Estate Preservation designation from the *Abts Institute for Estate Preservation*. Jeff also serves as a member of the Legal Council for The Estate Plan™, a nationally recognized estate preservation company headed by Henry Abts, trust guru and author of *The Living Trust*.

In addition to working on Care Assistance Planning as both an Attorney and as a Care Planner in Raleigh, NC since 1996, Mr. Marsocci is the author of *The Anti-Probate Revolution*, *The IRA Trust*, and other planning books found on Amazon.com.

Mr. Marsocci frequently holds seminars for clients, financial advisors and attorneys on topics related to the Care Assistance Planning, legal estate planning, and financial aspects of legacy planning as well as developing and presenting continuing legal education courses for attorneys and life insurance agents. He and his wife Kathleen live in Raleigh, North Carolina and work with students on service leadership development and planning. Both are recipients of the President's Call to Service Award through the Points of Light Foundation for completing more than 4,000 hours of service during their lifetimes.

This book is dedicated to caregivers who sacrifice so much of themselves to help their loved ones.

TABLE OF CONTENTS

Introduction		1
Chapter One	Ten Myths of Care Assistance Planning	7
Chapter Two	Your Basic Care Options	15
Chapter Three	Ways to Pay for Long Term Care	21
Chapter Four	The Income Test	27
Chapter Five	Countable, Non-Countable and Exempt Assets	33
Chapter Six	The Five Year Rule, Snapshot Date, and Gifting Explained	41
Chapter Seven	Finding the Right Professional	49
Chapter Eight	The Veteran's Aid and Attendance Benefit	57
Afternote		63

Introduction

Thank you for reading this book on North Carolina Care Assistance Planning. There are many challenges in Care Assistance Planning (also called long term care planning and, more narrowly than the field deserves, Medicaid planning.) The government does not make it easy. I've been working in this field for more than 16 years now, and I can tell you the one thing that the government does NOT want you to know... that you do not have to go broke and lose everything to qualify for the government Care Assistance programs that you spent a lifetime paying into through taxes.

As an experienced planning professional in NC, I am happy to help you learn the basics of Care Assistance Planning BEFORE you begin rearranging assets. One thing I can tell you about Medicaid qualification specifically is that it is never simple and it is never a matter of taking the same three steps that everyone else does. Each situation is unique, and getting one little thing wrong can cause the entire plan to implode. Before we begin, I want to address something.

I know you have a lot of questions, and it is extremely important to ask these questions before taking action.

- How do people shelter a lifetime worth of assets when Medicaid and other offices seem to want people to be broke?

- Do people simply give everything away?
- Isn't it true that planning has to be done five years before nursing home care is ever needed?
- (For the kids) Is there anything I can do if Mom or Dad has to go into a nursing home in the next few weeks?
- How do I find a professional who actually knows their stuff?

I'm going to cover all of this and many other useful bits of information. As Medicaid is the Care Assistance topic people generally want answers to very quickly, I have divided the chapters into seven simple parts with the material more focused on Medicaid, but please do not think that is all Care Assistance is about. For example, did you know there are four basic ways to pay for long term health care? There is long term care insurance. However, many people consider it to be too expensive by the time they need it. Then there is a properly constructed and explained Care Assistance Plan unique to each situation. But there are third and fourth options. Most people choose one of them and it's deadly to a Care Assistance Plan.

There are specialized trusts that can help with Care Assistance Planning, but timing is everything, not all trusts are the same, and trusts may only be a small part of a comprehensive plan.

Did you know there are three main questions you should ask Medicaid Planning professional or attorney before you hire them? These three question show you without a shadow of a doubt if they have the knowledge to help you with your plans. Hire the wrong person and you and your family could run into problems.

These are just a few of the tips I'll provide in this book. Here's what we'll cover:

Chapter 1: *Ten Myths of Care Assistance Planning.* Nearly everyone I have spoken to believes one or more of these myths are absolutely true, and it can put your home and your life savings at risk.

Chapter 2: *Your Basic Care Options.* There are four basic care options when it comes to long term care planning. In many cases, people will go through more than one type of care during life, but it is important to know the different options as well as the pros and cons of each.

Chapter 3: *Ways to Pay for Long Term Care.* There are four main ways to pay for long term care, and the right kind of financial and legal planning well in advance can make all of the difference in the world. But even in cases when there is not a lot of time, you can often preserve substantial assets for your loved ones.

Chapter 4: *The Income Test*, and how the North Carolina Medicaid offices look at income for individuals and married couples. While the rules are complex, there is actually a very simple answer to how your income affects Medicaid qualification in North Carolina.

Chapter 5: *Countable, Non-Countable and Exempt Assets* and an explanation of limits for North Carolina. How your assets are looked at for Medicaid qualification in North Carolina, and while it appears you have to be broke or nearly broke to qualify for Medicaid (or the Aid and Attendance Veterans Benefit), there are many ways to maximize assets and minimize a spend-down for you and your family.

Chapter 6: *The five year rule, snapshot date, and gifting explained.* Because of different federal rules for gifting for estate tax purposes and Care Assistance qualification, taking steps on your own can be deadly to your overall plan, and the five-year rule is not as simple as it sounds. *Hint One*: You and your family can be in big trouble if you think you can gift away $13,000 or $14,000 a year and still qualify for Medicaid. *Hint Two*: If you think the longest you can be disqualified for Medicaid because of gifts is five years, you may also be in big trouble.

Chapter 7: *Finding the Right Professional and a Good Plan.* The three questions that can help you find the right professional. Because there are more than 200,000 rules for Medicaid-based Care Assistance alone and everyone's assets are different, this lesson comes with a big disclaimer that this is not a guideline to creating your own plan. In fact, it is our personal guarantee that simply copying what others have done will lead to you being disqualified for Medicaid assistance or wasting a lot of money.

Chapter 8: *The Veteran's Aid and Attendance Benefit.* A special form of Care Assistance available to Veterans, their spouses, and their widows and widowers based on income and medical expenses. While this benefit has certain restrictions, it may make all of the difference in the world.

While all of these chapters provide good information, each is only a small part of the vast puzzle that is Care Assistance Planning. In fact, these eight parts only scratch the surface. For legal and regulatory reasons, we have to provide a disclaimer that all of these materials are not advice, but here are two pieces of actual, direct advice that I will unequivocally stand behind:

1) DON'T TAKE PIECEMEAL ACTIONS ON YOUR OWN BECAUSE IT CAN CAUSE AN UNCHANGEABLE DISASTER; and

2) GET HELP FROM PROFESSIONALS.

Hopefully this information will prove useful to you, but in the meantime take notes. Working with a good team of professionals can make all of the difference, and you should line up any important questions you may have before you meet with them. If you are a resident of North Carolina and have questions, then please call me at The NC Care Assistance Center at 919-374-0694.

Chapter One:
Ten Myths of Care Assistance Planning

A few months ago, a family came in to ask for help with getting their mother approved for Medicaid. I had actually spoken with the three kids and Mom in 2008 when Mom was only in the beginning stages of Dementia. At that time, they decided to handle things on their own. Since then, Mom had declined and had recently been in the memory care unit of a nursing home for the last 5 months at $6,300 per month, and now that her assets were about to run out they wanted help with applying for Medicaid.

"We just need to make sure that we fill out the application correctly," the oldest daughter said. "I know we've done everything right up until now, but I know how critical the application is."

And so I started reading through the draft Medicaid application they had filled out, I got to the section on gifts, and I immediately knew there was a problem. Apparently, Mom had written checks for $13,000 to each child and grandchild for the past three years and $12,000 to each of them the year before. That's three children, four grandchildren, and a total of $357,000 transferred in the last four years. On top of that, Mom had also transferred her house to the youngest daughter.

"Why did your Mom write all of these checks?" I asked.

"Well, because she could and she needed to spend down her assets," the son said. "She gave each of us the maximum amount she could each year. That's right, isn't it?"

"Unfortunately, no," I replied. "Those are amounts exempt from federal gift tax, not from the gifting penalties under the Medicaid program."

"No, that can't be right," the oldest sister said, a look of panic starting to come over her. "Our neighbor works for an accountant and she told me that those gifts don't count."

"I'm sorry," I said. "Again, it doesn't count for gift TAX purposes, but it does count for Medicaid eligibility purposes. Let's hold that for a minute. What about the house being transferred to you?"

The youngest daughter spoke up. "Well, that should be OK," she said, trying to convince herself. "We were told that as a 'caretaker child' Mom could transfer the house to me. I helped her run errands, took her to doctor appointments, and even took out the trash because it was getting too difficult for her. That IS alright, isn't it?"

"How long did you live in the house with your mother?" I asked.

"Oh, I didn't live there," she said. "I was there at least two or three days a week, and then just about every day for a few hours when things started to get worse. That is OK, isn't it?"

I leaned back into my chair a little, bracing myself for the bad news I had to give. I started tapping in numbers into the calculator, figuring if I had to give bad news it should at least be accurate bad news. "Actually, the transfer of the house doesn't come under the caretaker child exception because you didn't actually live with your mother," I said. "But having the house won't disqualify your mother from getting Medicaid since it is worth only $200,000. We just have to transfer the house back to her. It does mean that Medicaid can put a lien on the house, but that is better than not getting Medicaid at all."

They looked a bit shocked, and I decided to just rip the bandage off. "If you don't, then she won't be eligible for Medicaid for 89 months, meaning 7 years and 5 months. If you do, then it is only 56 months or 4 years and 8 months. Is there any possibility all of the money she gifted to the family can be paid back."

"What are you talking about!" the son shouted. "We don't have that money anymore!"

"Hold on," the oldest sister said, quieting her brother. "Are you telling us that Mom won't be able to get Medicaid because of these gifts and moving the house to my sister?"

"Not for 89 months," I said. "Unfortunately, unless they are undone and the refunded money is spent down correctly, the effect of these transfers means you would be better off paying for your mother's care out of pocket for about the next four and a half years and then applying."

The youngest daughter then asked the million dollar question. (Well, not the million dollar question, but close enough). "So what would've happened if you had helped us plan for this when we came to you four years ago?" she asked.

"We probably could have saved more than $300,000 and protect the house from a Medicaid lien," I said.

They sat in silence.

There are a lot of myths surrounding the Care Assistance process, particularly when it comes to Medicaid since the program is the most complicated and skilled care is the most costly. And, unfortunately, the consequences of incorrect information are often irreversible and very, very expensive. That is why I have compiled the Top Ten Myths of Care Assistance Planning for you. If you believe even one of these is true, failing to get the right information and help can be catastrophic.

10 Myths That Can Put Your Home and Savings at Risk

Myth 10. *Medicare pays for all medical conditions, even ones lasting longer than 90 days*. The fact is that Medicare is a type of primary health insurance for seniors that takes care of a limited amount of services for a limited period of time. It does not pay for all long term care needs.

Myth 9. *Medicare Supplements pays for long term care*. While the various Medicare supplements pay for things that regular Medicare doesn't and can help defer out-of-pocket costs, it does not pay for long term care, which can be the most expensive cost to you and your family.

Myth 8. *Primary Health Insurance pays for long term care*. Just as with Medicare, even with all of the supplements, will not pay for long term care, neither does privately paid health insurance.

Myth 7. *If you need long term care, you can just buy Long Term Care Insurance at that point*. This is like saying you can always buy life insurance at a young age if you develop cancer. While it may actually be possible to find an insurance company to insure you, you better believe it will be astronomically expensive and you are better off getting it when you are healthy.

Myth 6. *You can qualify for Care Assistance by giving your assets away just before you go into a nursing home*. While there are certain Care Assistance benefits available to Veterans, their spouses, and widows/widowers, this is often for "non-skilled care" assisted living help. Simply giving all of your assets away can work if done more than five years before applying for Medicaid, but any sooner than that and you need a comprehensive Care Assistance Plan in place. And, no, there is no $14,000 a year per gifting exemption; that only relates to federal gift taxes and there is no similar exception for Medicaid.

Myth 5. *A revocable living trust protects assets from a Medicaid Spend Down*. While revocable living trusts are excellent estate planning tools and, in certain circumstances, can assist with a spend down for married couples, it does not simply exempt assets from a Medicaid spend down. In fact, it can even make otherwise exempt assets countable for Care Assistance purposes!

Myth 4. *You can help qualify for Care Assistance by signing over your house to your kids*. While there are many strategies that may include gifting assets, and even the house, to children, it is often the biggest and most financially crippling move you can make. Unfortunately, it is also one of the most frequent moves made by a family gripped by "nursing home panic" because they feel the need to do something, and there is no shortage of real estate attorneys who can draft a deed very inexpensively. And the good real estate attorneys (rightly) have waivers in their engagement letters absolving them from any liability.

Myth 3. *There's no need for a health care power of attorney or living will because the family knows what you want*. While this is also universally a good idea for estate and health planning purposes, it becomes all the more critical when long term care is involved. Having the right people in place at the right time to make health care decisions when you can't makes all the difference in the world. And having your end of life decisions regarding life support, artificial nutrition and hydration in a legally binding document means that your family doesn't have to guess or have the burden of such a monumental decision.

Myth 2. *Having a fill-in financial power of attorney from the office supply store or from a website is good enough*. It isn't. There are very specific gifting provisions, particular financial powers, and Care Assistance language that should be incorporated into financial power of attorney documents that relate to Care Assistance Planning. In fact, most estate planning attorneys do not have these provisions in their standard documents which may otherwise be very comprehensive.

Myth 1. *There's no need for a comprehensive Care Assistance Plan… my friend/ neighbor/ barista just did "X" and everything turned out OK*. There are more than 200,000 regulations surrounding the Medicaid portion of Care Assistance Planning (let alone other Care Assistance programs) and there are just as many combinations of strategies and techniques that can be used depending on you and your family's unique situation. It is a huge mistake to think that everything will be clear because you *think* you understand 3 pieces of a 200,000 piece puzzle. It's always best to have a comprehensive Care Assistance Plan in place before taking any actions.

With any luck, you have recognized some of these items as myths to begin with, but don't feel bad if you didn't. Care Assistance Planning is an extremely complicated area with an astounding number of traps and loopholes, and unless you make a career out of it you are not likely to know these myths from general reading and information from non-professionals. The main point I want to leave you with in this section is that Care Assistance Planning is far from simple. But, like the family in the beginning of the book, there can be a lot of savings for the family if planning is done correctly and a huge financial loss if done incorrectly.

Chapter Two: Your Basic Care Options

It's times like this that I really understood why it's important to have a support staff for Care Assistance Planning. While Jack (not his real name) was well organized, he knew he was in over his head and sought help. While Deana helped him organize some papers, Kathy brought him a glass of water and he was starting to look a little more at ease. Then he started in, talking faster than one of those disclaimers for a prescription drug you hear on the radio.

"Look, Jeff," Jack said. "I know that my Mom's going to need help, and it's going to cost money. I just don't know how much, and I need to make sure that her assets are going to last. I know there's some shifting around we can do with her accounts, but there seems to be so much conflicting stuff out there. What should we do?"

"Slow down for a moment," I said, holding my hand up and talking deliberately slower. "Before we go into any of that, how is your mom doing?"

Jack looked a little taken aback. "I… didn't really expect you to ask that," he said. "Other people I have spoken to didn't seem to know what they were talking about, but all they wanted to talk about was her assets."

I smiled. "It's a good thing you came here then," I replied. "Before we can do anything about your mom's assets, we need to make sure we know what kind of care she needs. While I want to know what the medical professionals think, I first want to know how you think your mom is doing. Is she in good spirits?"

Care Assistance Planning has to be about more than assets, income, and medical reports. Unfortunately, many professionals push those aside and focus only on the money. That is one reason we have a geriatric care manager provide an evaluation and care plan for all of our Care Assistance Planning clients, and, to the extent our clients allow, we involve the family as well. After all, the decision on a parent's long term personal care plan often involves the family as much as the parent.

The different options available relate often to what is referred to as the Activities of Daily Living as well as the Instrumental Activities of Daily Living. These are medical/health care evaluations more officially done by a medical professional when needed, but a quick evaluation by a geriatric care manager can help guide the big discussion of where is best for long term care needs. While each situation is different and there are many customized personal care plans, there are four main living options:

Option 1—Companion Care: Companion care is when someone comes in to the home to help you continue to live more or less independently but providing assistance only with those activities where help is needed. Companion care can run the gamut from preparing meals, house cleaning, shopping and errands, all the way to assistance with washing and dressing. Companion care can also range from full time to providing a supplement to help from the family. In a lot of cases, this is a first stage of care that may be replaced by a more structured living environment if illness progresses. In many other cases, it is only a temporary measure to assist someone who is convalescing until they regain strength and mobility.

Option 2—Move in with Family: While this is often a first reaction on the part of a family wanting to help as well as provide some cost savings, there are a lot of unanticipated difficulties. On the part of the person needing help, there are often strong emotional difficulties with having a lot of reliance on family members that they themselves used to take care of. Suddenly, the children that were dressed, fed, and bathed by a parent are now the ones doing the dressing, feeding and bathing, and that can be a tough thing for people to emotionally deal with. On the part of the children, there is often a huge disruption in their own lives and routines for work, school and activities for their kids, and other socializations that had been set for some time.

There is no doubt that this arrangement also has a lot of benefits, not the least of which is that the family is together during a time of difficulty and they can gain much emotional support from each other. And the cost savings compared to some of the other options is also a great benefit to the family. In some cases, moving in with the family has also been combined with the companion care option so that while family members are providing a lot of the needed care, there is someone else coming in to help with some of the activities that the parent would prefer to delegate to a non-family member, or, in some cases, cannot be done by a family member. In my own grandmother's case, she had moved in with my aunt when it was better that she not live alone anymore, but it reached a point when neither my aunt nor either of her two young sons could lift her from bed to a chair or from a chair to a walker without great difficulty.

Option 3—Assisted Living: Assisted living arrangements can range from simply living independently in a more communal environment where prepared meals and dining facilities are available along with organized activities all the way to needing some help with everything short of skilled nursing care. In many cases, assisted living facilities provide the whole range of assistance as needed so there is no need for someone needing more help to move out of the assisted living facility until it is time for more skilled medical care and assistance than the facility can provide.

Assisted living is often less expensive than nursing care, but it is still more expensive than independent living and certainly more expensive than moving in with family. However, there is definitely more that can be done for veterans, spouses of veterans, and widows/widowers of veterans when it comes to assisted living care, but that will be an educational section all on its own.

Option 4—Nursing and Skilled Care: This is often called nursing home care, but the fact is that it really is more accurate to call it "skilled care" because it can be administered in a facility or at home. Many people needing this level of care would prefer to stay at home, and it can be more cost-effective to do so. (When it comes to Care Assistance Planning and having Medicaid or other programs help pay for some of the care, the government is equally willing to have the lower costs of in-home but skilled care since it is cheaper for the government.) In other cases, a facility that provides skilled care may be exactly what it needed, and so staying at home may not medically be the best option for you or the family.

In any event, this is the level of care that often frustrates families the most because, unless they are medical professionals, the care of their loved one is taken largely out of their hands. Again, dealing with the loss of control is difficult for the individual needing care as well as the family, and this is one of the reasons we enlist a geriatric care manager for all of our Care Assistance Planning cases.

While most people come to us to help with the financial aspects of Care Assistance Planning, we have to start with what kind of care is required and preferred by our clients in order to achieve the best possible outcome. After all, saving money is and should be secondary to getting comfortable, competent and appropriate care.

Chapter Three:
Ways to Pay for Long Term Care

"Thank you for meeting with me," Fred said. "I really have no idea what is going on with Mom since Dad used to keep that all to himself."

Fred was meeting me for only the second time, and the first time was nothing more than a quick introduction over the Holidays so Fred would know where to go in case anything happened to his father and his mother was still in the nursing home.

"I'm afraid I'm pretty lost," Fred said. "The one thing I need to make sure is that Dad didn't somehow mess up Mom's Medicaid. I told the nursing home about Dad passing on, and they told me to call the Medicaid office because it may change her status. I called them and they said a lot of Dad's assets would have to be used to pay for her care. I decided to contact you before going down there."

"It's OK," I said. "You did the right thing meeting with me first. I've began working with your father for a few years now, just a few months before your mother went into the nursing home. He wanted to make sure that I ran through everything with you starting with the Care Assistance Plan we put together for them and let you know that there is nothing to worry about."

"But I know Dad more than a hundred thousand dollars, he had the house, and a lot of other possessions," he said. "That goes to Mom, doesn't it?"

"Actually, no," I responded. 'The accounts are already set to go into an irrevocable trust to take care of your mother without disrupting her Medicaid, and the house is already in that trust. Your father left nothing directly to your mother."

Fred looked confused.

"Here," I said, pulling out the original Care Assistance Plan. "Here's how we got here."

It's not the job of the Medicaid office personnel to save your family money. In fact, part of the Medicaid office's job is to advise you to pay for your own care as much as possible until your assets are gone and only then get you approved for the Medicaid Care Assistance program. So if you simply follow the government's advice in qualifying for Care Assistance, you'll end up paying for a lot more than you are legally obligated to.

There are four main ways to pay for long term care, and some are better than others depending on your situation.

Payment Method One: Personal Income

The first method of paying for long term care is simply by paying for it out of your own income. This means diverting some, most, or even all of your income to the care facility in order to cover the costs. While facility care varies greatly, the average month's stay in a skilled nursing facility in North Carolina is currently $6,300. For most individuals, this kind of income is not readily available, especially if there is a spouse outside the facility who needs some of the joint income for their monthly living expenses. Nonetheless, income is always considered the first way to handle paying for long term care, even if it does not cover the whole bill each month.

And so people can work their whole lives to earn a pension, reach the age to start social security, and with one bit of bad health it can all disappear. In many cases, even 100% of a person's income is diverted to a long term care facility to take care of them, it may still not be enough. That leads us to the second method of paying.

Payment Method Two: Liquidate Assets

In many cases, an individual or couple can spend their entire lives working hard, put money away, and then wish to leave the fruits of their labors to their children or other loved ones. Unfortunately, when it comes to expensive long term care, it can drain a lifetime of work in a few years or even months. Selling off stocks. Draining IRAs and 401ks. Cashing in savings bonds and CDs early. When not planned properly, it happens one month at a time all with the hope and prayer that you will get better. And then once you are better and can return home (if you haven't sold that to pay the bills), you may find most of your resources are gone and you have to live on a lot less.

Most of my clients don't like this option, and with good reason. After all, who wants one sickness to take away everything you've worked for and give it to a medical facility?

Payment Method Three: Long Term Care Insurance

A third method of paying for long term care is by purchasing long term care insurance. If you are still young and can afford to pay the premiums, then it is worth looking into. In addition to traditional long term care insurance, there are other insurance options that "add on" long term Care Assistance with some more traditional investments. However, it has become almost routine that the people who seek our help didn't purchase long term care insurance or did not purchase enough to cover all of the costs. And now that an illness is imminent, they are stuck being either uninsurable or the premiums are much more than they can afford.

A few years ago, a colleague told me about how he met with a client every year about his life insurance and investments, and every year he made the same suggestion. He told his client that if he passed on his wife would be able to continue in her same lifestyle without interruption because of the life insurance on him. However, the reverse wasn't true. If she passed on and he didn't have her pension and social security coming in, he would not be able to retire. Ever. And so he kept suggesting to his client that he get life insurance on his wife only to get laughed off that "there was no way his wife was going to die before him." Then one day the client walked into his office and said he finally was ready to talk about life insurance for his wife… because she was just diagnosed with stage 3 terminal cancer. Of course, life insurance was now out of the question. It is often worse when it comes to long term care insurance. While everyone realizes they will pass on one day, the thought of not being healthy enough to take care of yourself is almost unthinkable until it happens.

Payment Method Four: Care Assistance

There are various programs run through federal, state, and possibly local agencies designed specifically to help people pay for long term care. While this sounds great to many people faced with losing all of their income and assets to the nursing home (and also finding that long term care insurance is not an option), qualifying for these programs can be very complex. Especially if you want to save some of your assets for your family and/or make sure some of your income is available to support a spouse.

For Medicaid in particular, there are more than 200,000 rules that are changing all the time. And as you read in the Section "10 Myths That Can Put Your Home and Savings at Risk," there's no one or two easy solutions to qualify other than spending down everything first. Fortunately, there is help to gain Care Assistance if you work with the right professionals and follow the right, planned steps for your particular situation.

There are four main ways to pay for long term medical care, but as you've read most people would prefer to save something for themselves for when they get out of a facility or to save for the family when they pass on. There is no need to go completely broke to qualify for Care Assistance, but like most things in life it is not always easy to get the help you need without working with the right professionals.

Chapter Four: The Income Test

I ran into Mom and her daughter at the grocery store, which is unusual for us since we usually do the weekly shopping very early on Saturday morning, and the place is pretty empty at that hour. This time Fran and her daughter Doris (not their real names) needed some key ingredients for that afternoon's lunch that they forgot.

"Oh, Mr. Marsocci!" Fran said seeing me. "It's good to see you. I didn't know Care Assistance Planners shopped for groceries!"

We all laughed at that.

"It's good to see you, too," I said. "How's Don doing?"

"He's doing well," Fran said. "In fact, we're making an apple pie for lunch, and then we'll bring him a few slices tonight. It's still his favorite."

"I still can't thank you enough for helping Mom and Dad," Doris said. "Thanks to you, Dad is still in the nursing home doing reasonably well, and Mom has enough money each month to get by. If it weren't for your help, Mom would have been on food stamps and keeping the heat turned off in the winter."

"You're very welcome," I said. "I only helped your Dad qualify for the assistance he deserved, and I helped your Mom keep all of the income she was entitled to."

The rules surrounding income seem extraordinarily straightforward, but there are also some tremendous but hidden opportunities, particularly when a spouse outside of the care facility is involved and we're trying to qualify for Medicaid assistance. Today, we'll look at the income requirements when it comes to both individuals and spouses as well as some of the opportunities to divert income to a spouse. We won't get too deep into these opportunities because it can take hours upon hours to explain and all situations are different. If you need further information, then please give us a call.

Individual Income Test

As strange as this sounds, there really isn't an income test for individuals in North Carolina. That's right, the Medicaid office doesn't really care how high an individual's income is when it comes to Medicaid in the Care Assistance Planning context.

Why?

It's because, with a few exceptions, all of the individual's income goes to pay the facility first and then Medciaid picks up the difference. If an individual's assets are below the necessary limit and they medically qualify for Medicaid assistance, then it doesn't matter if the income of the individual is $500 a month or $,5,000 a month since it is essentially all going to pay for care.

Here are a few exceptions when an individual gets to keep some of their income:

- A personal needs allowance
- Necessary medical expenses outside of what Medicaid pays for
- Health insurance premiums

Other than that, the income of an individual has to be paid to the facility for long term care. While there does not appear to be much sense in putting together a complete Care Assistance Plan for an individual when reviewing the income requirements, the real savings for the family lies with the asset portion of plan. But when it comes to married couples, there is a world of difference when it comes to how income is treated in a Care Assistance Plan.

When one spouse needs long term care and has to qualify for Care Assistance through Medicaid, then we start with all of that spouse's income going towards their care. The spouse outside of the facility does not have to divert any of their income to paying for their spouse's care. Let me say that again:

The spouse outside of the facility does not have to divert any of their income to paying for their spouse's care.

Many times in the Care Assistance process and qualifying for Medicaid, people misread the income requirement regulations for something called the Minimum Monthly Maintenance Allowance (MMMA) for a spouse outside of a facility and assume that that is all the income *the spouse* can keep each month. However, that truly is a minimum income each month that the spouse is entitled to. If their income is less than that minimum, then they are entitled to divert some of their spouse's income away from the facility and to themselves in order to meet that minimum.

For example, let's assume that Fred needs skilled nursing care in a facility, and his wife Wilma does not. Here are the figures. (Please note that the Monthly Minimum Maintenance Allowance figure is completely made up because the actual number is always subject to change and varies from state to state):

Fred's monthly income:	$1,700
Wilma's monthly income:	$450
Monthly Minimum Maintenance Allowance:	$650

Based on these figures, since Wilma's income falls short of the monthly minimum amount by $200, she is allowed to keep $200 of Fred's income each month. While this is simple arithmetic, there are also ways to increase the monthly minimum maintenance amount if actual living expenses are higher. This includes potentially boosting the amount of monthly income kept because of energy costs, rent/mortgage, and other items that could be uncovered in a Care Assistance Plan. This can make all of the difference in the world to a spouse still living at home without sufficient income of their own to draw upon.

While this describes the minimum income for a spouse outside of a facility, there is no maximum income that spouse can keep each month, and here is where there are tremendous opportunities to divert income. Imagine if the situation was the same as above for Fred and Wilma, but in this process we were able to get Wilma another $500 in income each month in executing a comprehensive Care Assistance Plan. That would give Wilma $950 each month instead of only the minimum of $650. Wouldn't that make Wilma's life much easier? We'll talk about this process a little more in the next few sections on assets and qualifying for Care Assistance.

Chapter Five:
Countable, Non-Countable and Exempt Assets

I meet with people all of the time who have loved ones that will need skilled nursing care, but, like deer caught in headlights, they are too uncertain to make any move at all. As months go by, the family loses opportunities to plan, and the options in a properly constructed Care Assistance Plan dwindle until the "planning ahead" becomes "crisis planning." While there is still a tremendous amount we can do to save money for the family in a crisis situation, it pales in comparison to what can be saved when there is more time.

Take Mr. Johnson, for example. I met with him when his wife was initially diagnosed with the beginning stages of dementia but was still able to get around. I laid out what we offer in the form of a comprehensive Care Assistance Plan, but he wanted to try doing it himself. I heard about a year and a half later that he declared bankruptcy because he had tried to accomplish a spend down on his own, ended up mortgaging his home and farm to comply with the Medicaid rules, and then didn't have enough money to pay both the mortgage and his other bills. While we didn't do a Care Assistance Plan for him and his wife, I know that we would have been able to set things up so he would have been able to keep the home and farm, have enough monthly income to handle all of his debts and expenses, allow him to have more than $100,000 in assets in his own name, and transfer at least $50,000 more to his children. Because of Mr. Johnson's case, we decided to put in place a Care Assistance Plan guarantee that any plan we create will save at least three times the cost of the care plan over a one year period.

But what needs to be looked at for a good Care Assistance Plan? How are assets classified and so much money saved for the family? Here are the types of assets, and in the next section we will review some of the boundaries surrounding the techniques we employ. As an important note, these classifications are also important when it comes to Care Assistance Planning for the Veterans Aid and Attendance benefit although the boundaries for the VA benefit are different than Medicaid-based Care Assistance Planning.

Countable Assets

Countable assets are the most common assets people want to be able to preserve apart from sentimental, personal items. These are generally the liquid assets that people own that can be converted to cash easily. Consequently, these are the types of assets in a Care Assistance Plan that need to be spent down to the appropriate limits, or converted to assets that are exempt or not counted. For example, the following are considered countable assets:

- Cash, checking, savings, money market, and CDs
- Stocks, bonds, mutual funds, brokerage accounts
- IRAs, 401ks, 403bs, SEP IRAs, Keough Plans, and other retirement plans with a balance (as opposed to monthly

pension payments that come to you for life; that is considered income and not an asset)

- The cash value of life insurance and annuity balances (meaning the annuity has not been annuitized yet)
- All autos, trucks, boats, machinery, etc. beyond the first automobile
- Real estate beyond what is Exempt or Unavailable
- Any other deposits that can be accessed or refunded if not used, such as retirement community "buy-ins", pre-paid rent, pre-paid utilities, etc.

Basically, if you can access it and easily convert it to cash (or even not so easily in the case of real estate), then it counts towards the limits you are allowed to keep, or you and a spouse are allowed to keep, and any excess must be spent, converted, or gifted appropriately in coordination with a Care Assistance Plan. (NOTE: DO NOT JUST START GIFTING ASSETS. THIS IS ONE REASON PEOPLE GET IN FINANCIAL TROUBLE).

Non-Countable/Unavailable Assets

In addition to Countable Assets, there are also assets that are Non-Countable, or better known as "Unavailable" Assets. In these instances, they may be assets that would normally be countable but for some reason are not immediately available or easily liquidated. These assets are:

- An inheritance prior to it being distributed to you

- Lawsuit proceeds before the judgment is collected and distributed to you
- Jointly-owned real estate that would cause an undue hardship to the other owner or other real estate with a legal impediment that makes it hard or impossible to sell
- Other property rights that cannot be liquidated, such as a "life estate" (a lifetime right to live on the property without actually owning the property)

The key to the unavailable assets category is that there is no way to actually get cash from the asset now. In other words, you cannot be denied Care Assistance because you are going to get a large inheritance when an estate settles. However, once the estate assets are in your possession, they end up becoming countable (or possibly Exempt) assets. Some of our Care Assistance Planning techniques involve making countable assets get tied up legally to become unavailable.

Exempt Assets

Exempt Assets are the third and most important category when it comes to a Care Assistance spend-down, because these are otherwise countable assets that you get to keep. The list is different for individuals versus couples, and so we'll break this into two lists.

For Individuals

- Cash in the amount of $2,000 or less
- The home with about $500,000 in equity (again, we're not going to use exact numbers because these can change quickly). There are some major restrictions on the home that are beyond the scope of this section and you should discuss it with a professional.
- One Automobile (again, within certain restrictions)
- Personal Property, such as clothing, furniture, electronics, and jewelry (to an extent)
- Funeral account, burial insurance, and burial spaces (within limits, and for the burial spaces, potentially also for immediate family members)
- Life insurance with no cash value (or with the cash value counted as part of the $2,000)
- Certain other assets that are more appropriate for a conversation at our office

For Married Couples

- Cash in the amount of $2,000 or less for the spouse needing care; cash in the amount of approximately $100,000 or less for the spouse not needing care
- The home with an unlimited equity value. There are some major restrictions on the home that are beyond the scope of this section and program that we can address at our office.

- One Automobile (again, within certain restrictions)
- Personal Property, such as clothing, furniture, electronics, and jewelry (to an extent)
- Funeral account, burial insurance, and burial spaces (within limits, and for the burial spaces, potentially also for immediate family members)
- Life insurance with no cash value (or with the cash value counted as part of the $2,000)
- Certain other assets that are more appropriate for a conversation at our office

These are the three main categories of assets that we need to deal with in a good Care Assistance Plan. In most cases, we want to maximize the Exempt assets, plan for the Non-Countable/Unavailable assets, and restructure or transfer the Countable Assets to get them below the limits for Exempt assets. As I discussed in the introductory chapter, there is no way that I can teach you enough to be able to put together a good Care Assistance Plan on your own, but at least I can give you enough information to understand the basics and, hopefully, convince you to work with a competent professional as soon as possible instead of trying it on your own or putting it off to another day.

Unlike other areas of life and the law, there are very few mulligans or "take-backs" to try it again once a mistake is made in Care Assistance Planning. And these mistakes can cost into the hundreds of thousands of dollars.

Chapter Six:
The Five Year Rule, Snapshot Date, and Gifting Explained

Sometimes there is just nothing I can do, but it is almost always after the fact. Paul is one of those people who thinks he knows everything, and he was unfortunately finding out that he didn't know nearly as much about Care Assistance Planning as he should. And now his Mom, well into Alzheimer's, was going to be caught without money to pay for her care.

In addition to confusing the $14,000 a year gift tax exemption with being exempt for Medicaid purposes, he filled out a Medicaid application for his mother 4 years and ten months after transferring Mom's house and most of her assets to him and his two sisters. Since he had heard it takes at least two months to get Medicaid approved, he filed the Medicaid application two months before the five year look back period expired… and was now told that she would not be eligible for Medicaid for another seven years and three months.

"I don't understand this!" he shouted. "It's only supposed to be five years, and she only had two months to go. We've been paying for her care out of the money she gave us almost five years ago except for the $13,000 exempt gifts each year. I planned this out to the last penny, and now you're telling me it's worse than if I did nothing?"

"Unfortunately, that is the case," I said. "The five year rule is very strict and often confusing for people who don't work in the Care Assistance field. The Medicaid office will look back five years from the date of application for gifts, but the period of ineligibility can actually be much longer than that. In this case, the gifts you scheduled out amounted to more than seven years of ineligibility for Medicaid. If you had waited two months to apply, the large gifts from almost five years ago would have been exempt and only the $14,000 gifts would have been counted. That would have cut back on the ineligibility period significantly, but not completely."

"But I thought those gifts didn't count!" Paul said.

"They don't count for Federal Gift Tax purposes, but they very much count for Medicaid purposes," I said. "It's a common mistake, but one that Medicaid is not forgiving about."

"So what am I supposed to do?" Paul asked.

"There are a few options we can pursue, but they all involve going to court," I said. "Is it possible for you and your sisters to just pay for Mom's care?"

Paul sunk into the conference room chair and sighed. "My sisters are going to kill me," he mumbled.

While there are tremendous Care Assistance Planning opportunities to save some assets for the family, it has to be done correctly, and there is a lot of misinformation surrounding some of the Medicaid rules. Here are the three most prevalent but misunderstood rules of Medicaid qualification.

Rule One: The "Snapshot" Date

The snapshot date is simply the date that the person entered the nursing home, and therefore is "locked in" to how their assets were arranged at that time. This is one of the reasons why it is so critical to get a good Care Assistance Plan in place before someone actually is in the nursing home and facing a giant financial burden. This is particularly true when a couple is involved because it can greatly affect how much in assets and income can be diverted to the spouse. Here's an Example:

Rory needs nursing home care and his wife Amy is trying to rearrange his assets to help. If Rory enters the nursing home on April 1 and Amy starts looking at their assets on April 3, they look like this:

- House worth $500,000
- Rory has IRAs, stocks, and cash worth $100,000
- Rory has income of $2,000 per month
- Amy has IRAs, stocks, and cash worth $50,000
- Amy has income of $700 per month

Based on these facts, Amy gets some help with putting together their finances and eventually qualifying Rory for Medicaid. In the end with a good Care Assistance Plan, Amy gets to keep about $75,000, she gets to keep the house with some repairs and upgrades, gets all burial and funeral expenses pre-arranged and paid for, and managed to get income of $2,500 per month to Amy. The downside is that she had to spend about $20,000 on Rory's care before Medicaid took over, and Amy does not get to have the maximum "Community Spouse Resource Allowance" of about $110,000.

Now let's take a look at the same facts but Amy starts planning a few months before Rory actually has to go into a nursing home. By shifting assets around prior to the snapshot date and using a simple revocable living trust on a temporary basis, the full $110,000 can be kept by Amy on the Snapshot Date, still take all of the same other spend down steps, but now Amy and Rory didn't have to spend down anything on Rory's care and still get all of the other benefits to Amy. In the end, Amy and Rory came out $55,000 ahead simply by planning two months out.

How is this possible? Why is it this way? It's because North Carolina and a lot of other states will allow the spouse outside the nursing home, frequently called the "community spouse", to have UP TO about $110,000 of assets, but it is not done by simply transferring the assets to the community spouse. It's done by taking the whole of the cash assets, dividing by two, and seeing how much the community spouse and the spouse in the nursing home get to keep. Again, a good but simple technique using a simple revocable living trust in conjunction with timing the snapshot date made a world of difference.

Rule Two: The Five Year Rule

This is probably one of the most misunderstood rules around. The five year "look back" period refers to how far back Medicaid will look in Care Assistance Planning to see if there were any gifts or transfers that would trigger a period of ineligibility. Let's take a look at what the Five Year Rule does mean before showing what it doesn't mean.

It DOES mean:

- Have the Medicaid office look back five years from the date of application to see if there were any gifts made
- Imposes a period of ineligibility for all collective gifts made within the five years before the date of application
- The period of ineligibility is the sum of those gifts divided by the cost figure determined by the Medicaid office to be a "monthly average cost" of skilled nursing home care (currently about $6,000) to come out to a number of months of ineligibility. (See below in the rule on gifting for an example).
- The period of ineligibility begins from the date of application

It DOES NOT mean:

- Mean that the maximum period of ineligibility is five years; it can be much more
- Mean a gift of $6,000 a year ago already expired because the ineligibility month started when the gift was made (it used to be that way, but it is not under current law)

The five year rule can be a little tricky and can profoundly and negatively impact planning. As you saw in the story at the start of this section, not understanding the fine points can lead to much more than five years before Medicaid Care Assistance Planning starts.

Rule Three: Gifting

Gifting can be an important and effective technique in Care Assistance Planning, but it has to be done in absolutely the right way. Even more important to understand, gifting within five years of applying for Medicaid Care Assistance is not necessarily a bad thing. In fact, many "crisis" Care Assistance Plans we develop include a lump sum gift with an accompanying ineligibility period, applying for Medicaid to get the period of ineligibility started, and then having the family take over paying for care during that period of ineligibility because the net gain to the family (along with the other spend down techniques) still has the family come out ahead.

Probably the biggest misconception around gifting is something I already mentioned: the annual amount of gifting excluded from gift taxes is not excluded from Medicaid scrutiny. The $13,000 amount most people have heard about (which jumped to $14,000 January 1, 2013) only relates to federal gift taxes. It has nothing to do with Medicaid. Another piece of that same misconception is that if the gifts are spread out among a lot of different relatives, then the implications are diluted. Again, this relates to the federal gift tax in that you can give $100,000 as 10 gifts of $10,000 each and it is not gift taxable, but there would be gift tax implications if you just gave one $100,000 gift to a person. As far as Medicaid is concerned, there is no difference since it counts up the total gifts given within the last five years regardless of the recipient or recipients (excepting spouses).

Care Assistance Planning can have a huge impact on the family and a spouse staying out of the facility. Unfortunately, doing Care Assistance Planning the wrong way can also have a huge impact on the family if done incorrectly and not for the better.

Chapter Seven: Finding the Right Professional

I sat across from them over charity hotdogs and salad, enjoying the summer evening weather and the fact that the speeches were over. Unfortunately, the couple knew I worked in the Care Assistance field and wanted to chat about how great their life insurance person was.

"Oh, he was fantastic," he said. "Our insurance agent managed to get my mother a whole bunch of money more in income every month, funded a life insurance policy, and actually got a great deal on a mortgage for the house."

"A mortgage for the house?" I asked. "It was your father who went into the nursing home, right? Why did your mother need a mortgage if she had a lot of income coming in and the house was paid up?"

"Well, you know," she said as if it were the most obvious thing in the world. "To get more money out of the house to get a bigger life insurance policy. When my mother-in-law passes on, it will leave the family with a lot more money."

"What about your mother-in-law?" I asked. "How much did she get to keep in investments?"

"Well, not much," he said. "She has to keep her checking account below $2,000, right?"

"You mean, your father has to keep his account below $2,000," I said. "What about your mother?"

"Well, she does, too," he said, looking at his wife. "That's one of the things that made it so difficult. When Mom had to redo the roof, we had to pay for it and now she's paying us back a little bit each month. Usually she has to go out of her way to spend a lot of money to keep her account low enough each month, but not when the roof happened."

Now I saw what was going on. Insurance is only one part of an overall plan, but there are some insurance salesmen who only think of their commissions. This one maxed out his commission by having the clients needlessly sell off everything to pay the premium on an annuity, and then went back for more by having the mother pull all of the money out of the house to buy an insurance policy.

"Here," he said, pulling out the insurance agent's card. "You might want to work with him."

"Thanks," I said, taking the card with a smile, thinking I'll now know who to stay far, far away from.

There are many different ways to screen Care Assistance Planners, and there are always personal questions people want to ask relevant to their own situation. One of the most important choices a family can make is to choose a Care Assistance Planner who will lead the team of professionals helping them and their loved ones. While questions about your personal situation are always important and should be asked, there are also all of the usual questions about experience and education people ask as if they were interviewing someone for a job.

I was once pressed by a colleague to come up with three and only three questions that will show whether or not a professional knows what they are talking about when it comes to Care Assistance Planning. After all, the insurance agent in the above story probably helped hundreds of clients and their families. He may have even gone to some top schools. But clearly the only thing he knew about Care Assistance Planning was how to make money. He didn't know or care about maximizing benefit, flexibility, and quality of life for the family. Until a Care Assistance Planner knows more about your situation, some preliminary questions can help test their ability.

Here are the three questions (along with the frustrating, but correct, answers) to ask when screening a Care Assistance Planner:

Question One: Can you use a revocable living trust to qualify for Medicaid/Care Assistance?

Horrible Answer: "Yes, anything you put into a revocable living trust is exempt from a Medicaid spend down." This is about as wrong as you can get. In the estate planning arena, a revocable living trust is a wonderful tool for avoiding probate, but it does nothing to avoid the assets in the trust from being looked at for Medicaid or other benefit programs. The reason this is so is because the grantor setting up the trust maintains control over the assets. There are also other kinds of trusts that may be very useful in qualifying for Care Assistance programs while retaining assets in them, but those are typically irrevocable trusts where you have to give up control and usually do so five years in advance.

Bad Answer: "No, there is no way to use a revocable living trust in the Medicaid/Care Assistance process." While this is not as bad of an answer as the one above, it does show that the professional does not truly understand all of the tools and rules involved in Care Assistance Planning. A revocable living trust can, in fact, be an important tool in Care Assistance Planning, but it is not a cure all, nor is it a forbidden entity. Which leads us to…

Good Answer: "It depends." The reason this is the best answer is that a revocable living trust can be used in conjunction with some of the Medicaid qualification rules to save money for a spouse not going into the nursing home (often called the "community spouse"). Since all assets in a revocable living trust are considered countable assets, the trust can be used to first raise the countable assets as high as they can be for the community spouse before shifting, spending and gifting strategies can get to qualification. Recently we helped a client who worked with another Care Assistance Planner, and using a revocable living trust allowed us to plan out an additional $80,000 in savings beyond the other professional's plan for the husband whose wife needed skilled nursing care.

Question Two: Shouldn't I just gift assets right away to qualify for Medicaid/Care Assistance?

Horrible Answer: "Yes, absolutely. If you gift everything away today, then tomorrow you can apply for Medicaid and qualify." As you've already read previously, this can be one of the worst things you can do resulting in sometimes even more than five years of ineligibility.

<u>*Bad Answer*</u>: "Absolutely not! Unless you have five years, you should never make any gifts." While not as bad as the horrible answer, it cuts off what can be an important tool in the overall Care Assistance Planning process. Simply throwing out that tool is not a good idea.

<u>*Good Answer*</u>: "It depends." If there are five years… or even less but still a good amount of time… gifting can be a good part of an overall strategy. While there is often some insurance and other shifting of assets to be done, depending on the assets and condition, gifting to family members and loved ones may be one component of an overall Care Assistance Plan. For example, if an individual has taken all other steps possible in Care Assistance Planning and still has $126,000 left to spend down, gifting all of it to his children would result in 20 months of ineligibility, but that may not be so bad. For 20 months, the kids do not have to spend the entire cost of the care to the nursing home... because Dad's income each month is also going to the nursing home. If Dad has $2,000 per month in income, and nursing care costs $6,300 per month, then the children will actually get to keep $40,000 of Dad's money through the gifting strategy.

Question Three: Shouldn't I just buy long term care insurance?

Horrible Answer: "No, Long Term Care insurance is just an expensive scam. It's like throwing money down a hole." Long term care insurance… more specifically, the right long term care insurance for the right period of time… can be an extremely beneficial tool as part of an overall Care Assistance Plan.

Second Horrible Answer: "Yes, absolutely. Get the best, longest-lasting and highest payout long term care policy you can." Again, Long term care insurance… more specifically, the right long term care insurance for the right period of time… can be an extremely beneficial tool as part of an overall Care Assistance Plan. Yes, that was exactly the same sentence as above, because it is just as true that never having Long Term Care Insurance is just as bad an answer as always having a massive long term care insurance policy.

Good Answer: "It depends." Again, the non-definitive answer is the best. Buying long term care insurance may be good decision depending on the situation, and from there finding the right policy paying the right amount over the optimal period of time for your situation is critical. Even more, as time goes on, the policy may be amended and even decreased to fit changing needs.

As maddening as it is to some of my clients and their families, the best answer to all of these questions is "it depends." It's not very definitive, but it is the most accurate when the Care Assistance Planner is still in the interviewing phase. Until they have all of the information in front of them and have the ability to discuss things with the clients in more detail, there is no way to give a yes or no answer to any of these questions. If a professional at this stage is giving simplistic answers, you know you probably need to keep looking.

Chapter Eight:
The Veteran's Aid and Attendance Benefit

I get the question from time to time, and this seminar was no different. And as usual, I had to answer a question with a question:

Question: "You've been talking about Care Assistance Planning largely based on needing nursing home care and qualifying for Medicaid, but my father is having a hard time getting by with the cost of assisted living. It's different. Everyone I've talked to says Medicaid doesn't cover assisted living. Is there anything we can do?"

My Question: "Is your father a Veteran?"

"What difference does that make?"

"It could make a world of difference."

The Veteran's Administration has various programs that help Veterans with medical and other costs, but only in the right situations. Since Care Assistance Planning encompasses that certain Aid and Attendance pension benefit, we can and should discuss it.

The Aid and Attendance benefit is a very specific type of support to help Veterans, the spouses of Veterans, and the widows and widowers of Veterans with high medical costs and living expenses. This often happens in assisted living situations since the medical and living costs are high, but the type of care does not rise to the level of needing skilled nursing care.

Just as every situation is different when it comes to Medicaid qualification, it is also different in every situation with the Veteran's Aid and Attendance pension benefit. What makes it even more complicated, the asset test for an applicant is actually subjective. So while Medicaid has hard and fast numbers for qualification ($2,000 for an individual, etc.), the amount a Veteran and/or their spouse gets to keep is not exact.

In applying for the Aid and Attendance pension benefit, you always want to have a professional involved. Considering the complexity of this area alone, even I work with a separate Veteran's Benefit Consultant to create the specific plan and harmonize it with the rest of the Care Assistance Plan. However, here are the four big tests in qualifying for the pension:

Test One, Service Requirements: Before September 7, 1980, the veteran must have served on active duty for at least 90 days, one day of which must have been during war time. For Veterans who have served at some point during World War II through the end of Vietnam, it is extraordinarily hard not to qualify except in cases where service was only between Korea and Vietnam (served after January 31, 1955 but before February 28, 1961). After September 7, 1980, the Veteran must have served at least 24 months or for the full period called for active duty. The Veteran must also have an honorable discharge to qualify.

Test Two, Medical Needs Test: There are various situations where the pension benefit will apply. If the Veteran is under 65, then they must be completely and permanently disabled. If over 65, then there is no disability requirement, but the Veteran must be blind or nearly blind, a patient in a nursing home because of mental or physical incapacity, or (most often) proves a need for assistance in performing some or all of the basic functions of daily life including bathing, feeding, dressing, toileting, etc. known as activities of daily living. There is also consideration if the person is homebound.

Test Three, Income: The income test seems very simple, but it isn't. Using 2012 numbers, if an individual has less than $1,094 monthly income, then they can qualify. If it is a married couple, then the combined income level is $1,337 per month. These income levels are extremely low, and most people assume that they simply do not qualify. In fact, if they call the Veteran's Administration, they'd tell most callers they don't qualify. However, it is not that simple because unreimbursed medical expenses can be deducted from the income. Now, suddenly a lot more people fall below these income levels once the unreimbursed medical expenses are factored in. There are also some ways to pay family members for certain medical or nursing services, which may be a way to legitimately shift some assets to children or loved ones who are caregivers.

Test Four, Assets: Like Medicaid, there is a limit on the resources/assets that may be retained. Unlike Medicaid, there is no set number on this. The rules states "the market value, less mortgages or other encumbrances, of all real and personal property owned by the claimant, except the claimant's single dwelling, including a reasonable lot area, and personal effects suitable to and consistent with the claimant's reasonable mode of life."

There is no exact amount listed. However, the rules do also state the pension shall be denied "when the corpus of the estate of the veteran or, if the veteran has a spouse, the corpus of the estates of the veteran and the veteran's spouse is such that under all the circumstances, including consideration of the annual income of the veteran, the veteran's spouse, and the veteran's children, it is reasonable that some part of the corpus of such estates be consumed for the veteran's maintenance."

As with Medicaid, there are some exempt assets, but by and large assets greater than $80,000 are grounds for declining the pension. However, in many cases depending on the region and location of the applicant, much lower asset levels are required to qualify for the pension. Again, in the end, it is best to work with a Care Assistance Planner and Veteran's Benefit Consultant to help arrange your assets to qualify.

There are four tests for qualifying for the Veteran's Aid and Attendance pension benefit, but there is help for Veterans who need it. There are qualified professionals out there to help, but it certainly should be considered in the larger context of a good Care Assistance Plan.

Afternote

Thank you for reading this book on North Carolina Care Assistance Planning. Hopefully you have gained some valuable insight into the world of qualifying for assistance for long term care needs. However, this is not the end of looking for answers but only the beginning. From here, it is important to fight a very natural paralysis, get a little organized with your finances, and reach out to professionals that can help.

If you would like to talk to the author, you can reach him at The NC Care Assistance Center, LLC at 919-374-0694.

Made in the USA
Monee, IL
04 November 2026

67352868R00046